Digger, Dozer, Dumper

HOPE VESTERGAARD

illustrated by DAVID SLONIM

CANDLEWICK PRESS

Are you quick? Or slow and steady?
There's a truck for you.
Are you precise? Or really strong?
We've got work to do.
If you like to move and groove,
it's time to get in gear!
Trucks do important jobs each day—
come on, the gang's all here!

STREET SWEEPER

Early morning, empty streets.
His whir disturbs the hush.
Good-bye, grime!
It's cleanup time —
here comes the sweeper's brush.
His steely whiskers whisper
as they gather dust and dirt.
They tickle all the gutters,
then rinse them with a squirt.
He's quiet and determined.
He doesn't miss a spot.
And when the streets are tidy,
he'll clean the parking lot.

GARBAGE TRUCK

The garbage truck adores his work —
the sights, the smells, the sounds!
The sour milk, the clanging lids,
the clumpy coffee grounds.
Hydraulic arms reach out, then lift.
He hoists the bins up high,
then tips and dumps and shakes them out . . .
and BANGS them down — good-bye!

DUMP TRUCK

The dump truck doesn't dump his dirt
just anywhere —
he's precise.
He slowly lifts his giant bed
and checks his target twice.
CRASH! BANG! CLANGETY CLANG!
The gravel starts to spill —
a mighty swoosh, and just like that,
he pours a little hill.

BACKHOE

The backhoe's two machines in one:
a useful little truck.
His front end pushes dirt and rocks;
his back end digs out muck.

Who needs a steering wheel? Not her!
Two levers make her tires whir.
Both front: she goes.
Both back: retreat!
She zips and turns across the street.
One front, one back, steers left or right.
She spins and veers in corners tight.
But that's not all her levers do:
they scoop and lift and drill straight through.

EXCAVATOR

Who made this hole? A digger.
Too small? She'll make it bigger.
Too big? She'll fill that hole.
Big rocks? She'll make them roll.
Her name? The excavator.
Her job? Smooth operator.

BULLDOZER

The bulldozer isn't sleepy.
He's always in a rush.
He pushes piles of dirt and junk,
and levels trees and brush.
He's not a bully, either,
although he's big and tough.
He waits his turn, plays well with friends,
and pushes just enough.

CEMENT MIXER

Around
and around
and around it goes —
his iron belly's churning.
Around
and around
and around it flows —
the concrete must keep turning.
No time to wait;
he can't sit still.
He has to beg your pardon.
For if he dawdles on the way,
his slushy load will harden.

FIRE TRUCK

The fire truck comes dressed for work
with tons of handy tools.
Pumps and axes, lamps and poles,
and hoses hung on spools.
Extinguishers and breathing masks,
and boots and helmets, too.
A bench of seats and hang-on bars
to hold the rescue crew.
If firefighters need some help
to reach things way up high,
he opens up his ladder
and lifts them to the sky.

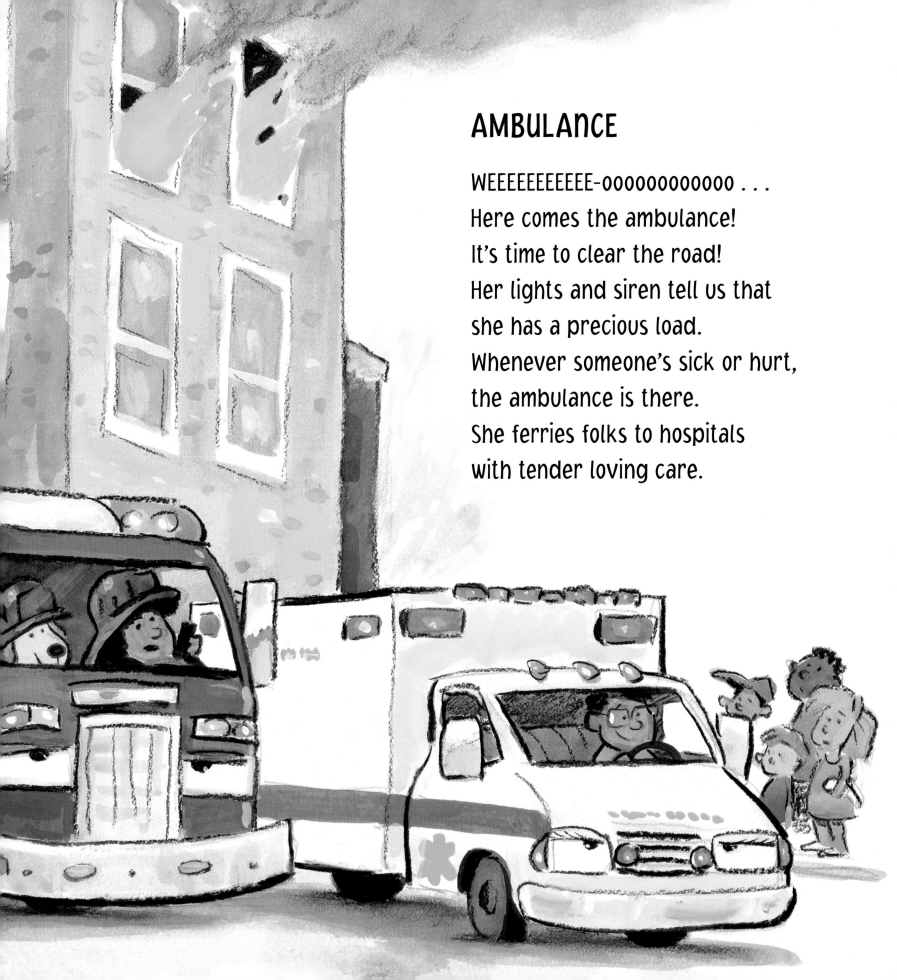

AMBULANCE

WEEEEEEEEEEE-ooooooooooooo . . .
Here comes the ambulance!
It's time to clear the road!
Her lights and siren tell us that
she has a precious load.
Whenever someone's sick or hurt,
the ambulance is there.
She ferries folks to hospitals
with tender loving care.

CHERRY PICKER

The cherry picker's lanky arm
unfolds into the air,
reaching high among the trees
to find what's lurking there:
a traffic light,
a broken branch,
a kite that lost its way,
a waving wire,
a pointy spire,
a lonesome little stray.
The picker pauses in the sky,
plucks its target,
then . . .
gently, slowly, gracefully
sets it down again.

TOW TRUCK

Out of gas? In a ditch?
Crashed and don't know which end's which?
Bent your fender? Lost your way?
Tow Truck's here to save the day.
She's got wrenches. She's got tires,
jumper cables, extra wires,
a winding winch to tug and tow,
and lots of horsepower . . . off you go!

STEAMROLLER

After the asphalt's dumped and spread
in sticky, long black lines,
the road must cure. You can be sure
Steamroller's close behind.
She's broad and big, a massive rig —
molasses slow, but steady.
And after she has barreled through,
the road is smooth and ready.

FORKLIFT

The forklift's snout pokes in and out
of pallets, piles, and crates.
Her L-shaped nose inspects the rows
and tallies all the freight.
Up and down, over and out,
then up and down once more.
She stacks and packs the merchandise
in warehouse, yard, and store.

SEMI

The mighty mover semitruck
has eighteen giant wheels.
He's strong and tall. He's built to haul
long trailers made of steel.
He's highway, byway royalty:
his cargo makes him king.
His shiny cab sits high and proud.
His tires hum and sing.
He rules the road. Each precious load
compels him to keep going.
So clear the way, or else you'll hear
his regal air horn BLOWING.
HOOOOOONK, HONK!

SNOWPLOW

When everyone else
is tucked in bed
beneath a winter blanket,
the snowplow truck
has just begun
to push and scrape and bank it.
In blowing squalls
or sleety storms,
the snowplow's making piles
of slush and snow that line the streets
for miles and miles and miles.

Digger, dozer, dumper, grader,
backhoe, roller, excavator,
cherry picker, double-decker,
concrete mixer, semi, wrecker.

Trucks that sweep and dig and shift.
Trucks that dump and tow and lift.
Hauling garbage, moving goods,
building houses, clearing woods.
Trucks as far as eyes can see . . .

Which truck would **you** like to be?

For Ben Bryant, excavator extraordinaire,
and for Emmett, Oscar, and Charlotte, who make my motor hum
H. V.

To Joey and Josiah
D. S.

Text copyright © 2013 by Hope Vestergaard
Illustrations copyright © 2013 by David Slonim

First edition 2013

Library of Congress Catalog Card Number 2012947724
ISBN 978-0-7636-5078-0

16 17 18 TLF 10 9

Printed in Dongguan, Guangdong, China

This book was typeset in Jacoby Light Condensed.
The illustrations were done in acrylic and charcoal on illustration board.

Candlewick Press
99 Dover Street
Somerville, Massachusetts 02144

visit us at www.candlewick.com